Social Media Advertising Mastery

Drive Results and Grow Your Business!

By

Joel K. John

Table Of Content

Understanding the Power of Social Media Advertising

In today's digital age, social media advertising has emerged as a powerful tool for businesses to connect with their target audience and achieve their marketing objectives. The widespread adoption of social media platforms has created a unique opportunity for businesses to reach a vast user base and engage with potential customers in a highly targeted and personalized manner.

One of the key reasons why social media advertising holds such power is its unparalleled reach. Platforms like Facebook, Instagram, Twitter, LinkedIn, and YouTube boast billions of active users worldwide. This extensive user base provides businesses with the potential to reach a diverse audience across various demographics, geographies, and interests.

With social media advertising, businesses can transcend geographical boundaries and connect with users from different parts of the world, enabling them to expand their reach and tap into new markets.

Another aspect that makes social media advertising powerful is the ability to precisely target specific audiences. Social media platforms collect vast amounts of user data, including demographics, interests, behaviors, and preferences. This data is leveraged by advertisers to create highly targeted and personalized campaigns. By utilizing advanced targeting options, businesses can narrow down their audience based on factors such as age, location, interests, job title, and more. This level of targeting precision ensures that businesses can deliver their ads to the most relevant audience, increasing the chances of capturing their attention and driving conversions.

Social media advertising also offers unparalleled engagement opportunities. Unlike traditional advertising channels, social media allows businesses to directly interact with their audience through comments, likes, shares, and direct messages. This engagement not only helps build brand loyalty and trust but also provides valuable insights into customer preferences and feedback. Businesses can leverage these insights to refine their advertising strategies, tailor their messaging, and deliver a more personalized experience to their target audience.

Additionally, social media advertising provides measurable results and a high return on investment (ROI). Unlike traditional advertising methods where it can be challenging to track the impact of campaigns, social media platforms offer robust analytics and tracking tools.

Advertisers can monitor key performance metrics, such as impressions, clicks, conversions, and engagement rates, in real-time. This data-driven approach enables businesses to optimize their campaigns, allocate budgets effectively, and achieve higher ROI by constantly refining their advertising strategies based on performance insights.

Benefits of Advertising on Social Media Platforms

Advertising on social media platforms offers a multitude of benefits for businesses seeking to enhance their marketing efforts and achieve their objectives.

In this section, we will explore some of the key advantages of leveraging social media advertising.

Extensive Reach: Social media platforms have billions of active users worldwide, providing businesses with unparalleled access to a vast audience. This reach allows businesses to connect with potential customers on a global scale, irrespective of geographical boundaries. Whether targeting a specific region or expanding into new markets, social media advertising offers the potential to reach a diverse and widespread audience.

Targeted Advertising: One of the most significant advantages of social media advertising is its advanced targeting capabilities. Social media platforms collect valuable user data, including demographics, interests, behaviors, and preferences. Advertisers can utilize this data to create highly targeted campaigns and ensure their ads are displayed to the most relevant audience. Precise targeting maximizes the chances of capturing the attention of potential customers who are more likely to be interested in the products or services being promoted.

Cost-Effectiveness: Compared to traditional advertising channels, social media advertising can be significantly more cost-effective. Many social media platforms offer flexible budgeting options, allowing businesses to set their desired ad spend and adjust it based on their specific needs and financial capacity. Additionally, the ability to target specific audiences minimizes wasted ad spend by ensuring that ads are shown only to individuals who are more likely to engage with them. This targeted approach helps optimize the return on investment (ROI) and makes social media advertising a cost-efficient option for businesses.

Engaging and Interactive Ads: Social media platforms provide an interactive environment where users actively engage with content. This presents businesses with an opportunity to create engaging and interactive ads that capture the attention of their target audience. Ad formats such as videos, carousel ads, polls, and interactive stories enable businesses to deliver immersive experiences that resonate with users and drive higher levels of engagement. The ability to interact with ads through comments, likes, shares, and direct messages also facilitates direct communication between businesses and potential customers.

Measurable Results and Analytics: Social media advertising offers robust analytics and tracking tools that provide valuable insights into campaign performance. Advertisers can track key metrics such as impressions, clicks, conversions, engagement rates, and more in real-time. This data-driven approach allows businesses to monitor the effectiveness of their campaigns, make data-backed decisions, and optimize their advertising strategies accordingly. The ability to measure results provides transparency and accountability, enabling businesses to continuously refine their efforts for better outcomes.

Brand Awareness and Customer Engagement: Social media platforms serve as hubs of social interaction and content sharing. Advertising on these platforms allows businesses to increase brand awareness and exposure to a wide audience. By consistently delivering valuable and engaging content, businesses can build brand loyalty and establish meaningful connections with their target audience.

Social media advertising also provides an avenue for direct engagement with customers through comments, messages, and reviews, fostering relationships and building trust.

Overview of Popular Social Media Platforms for Advertising

When it comes to social media advertising, there are several popular platforms that businesses can leverage to reach their target audience effectively. Each platform offers unique features, demographics, and user behavior patterns, making it essential for businesses to understand the landscape and choose the platforms that align with their advertising goals.

In this section, we will provide an overview of some of the most widely used social media platforms for advertising.

Facebook: With over 2.8 billion monthly active users, Facebook remains the largest social media platform. It offers a wide range of advertising options, including feed ads, stories, messenger ads, and more. Facebook's advanced targeting capabilities allow businesses to reach specific audiences based on demographics, interests, behaviors, and connections. It is an ideal platform for businesses targeting a diverse range of demographics and industries.

Instagram: Owned by Facebook, Instagram has quickly grown to become one of the most popular visual-centric platforms for advertising. It boasts over 1 billion monthly active users, with a significant focus on younger demographics and visually appealing content. Instagram offers various ad formats such as photo ads, video ads, carousel ads, and story ads. It is particularly effective for businesses with visually compelling products or services and those targeting younger audiences.

Twitter: Twitter is a fast-paced platform known for real-time updates, news, and trending topics. It has around 330 million monthly active users and is popular among users interested in current events, entertainment, and engaging in conversations. Twitter ads appear in users' feeds and can be targeted based on keywords, interests, demographics, and followers. It is suitable for businesses aiming to reach a highly engaged audience and participate in real-time conversations.

LinkedIn: LinkedIn is a professional networking platform with over 740 million members, primarily focused on business and career-related content. It offers advertising options like sponsored content, text ads, and sponsored InMail. LinkedIn's targeting capabilities revolve around professional criteria, such as job title, industry, company size, and skills. It is ideal for B2B businesses, recruitment efforts, and professional services targeting a professional audience.

YouTube: As the largest video-sharing platform, YouTube has over 2 billion logged-in monthly users. It offers various ad formats, including skippable and non-skippable video ads, display ads, overlay ads, and sponsored cards. YouTube ads can be targeted based on demographics, interests, and contextual relevance. It is suitable for businesses with video content and those looking to leverage the power of video advertising to engage with a wide audience.

TikTok: TikTok is a rapidly growing platform focused on short-form videos, with over 1 billion monthly active users. It is particularly popular among younger demographics and offers unique advertising options, including in-feed ads, branded effects, and branded hashtags. TikTok's algorithm-driven content discovery enables businesses to reach a wide audience and drive engagement through creative and entertaining video content.

It's important to note that this overview is not exhaustive, and there are several other social media platforms that businesses can explore for advertising, such as Pinterest, Snapchat, and Reddit. The choice of platforms should be based on factors like target audience demographics, user behavior, advertising objectives, and the nature of the business or industry.

Defining Your Advertising Goals and Objectives

Before embarking on a social media advertising campaign, it is essential for businesses to clearly define their advertising goals and objectives. Setting specific and measurable goals not only helps align advertising efforts with overall marketing strategies but also provides a framework for evaluating campaign success. In this section, we will explore the importance of defining advertising goals and objectives and provide insights on how to establish them effectively.

Aligning with Business Objectives: Advertising goals should be closely aligned with the broader objectives of the business. Whether the aim is to increase brand awareness, drive website traffic, generate leads, boost sales, or promote a new product or service, it is crucial to ensure that advertising goals directly contribute to the overarching business goals. This alignment ensures that advertising efforts have a meaningful impact on the bottom line and help move the business forward.

Specificity and Measurability: Effective advertising goals should be specific and measurable. Vague or general goals make it difficult to track progress and determine the success of the campaign. For example, instead of setting a goal to "increase brand awareness," a specific and measurable goal would be to "increase brand awareness by 20% among the target audience within six months." Specific goals provide clarity and allow for meaningful evaluation of campaign performance.

SMART Goal Framework: The SMART framework is a useful approach to set goals that are specific, measurable, achievable, relevant, and time-bound. Following this framework ensures that goals are well-defined and provide clear direction for advertising campaigns. SMART goals are:

Specific: Clearly define the desired outcome and focus of the advertising efforts.

Measurable: Establish specific metrics and key performance indicators (KPIs) to track progress and success.

Achievable: Set goals that are realistic and attainable within the available resources and timeframe.

Relevant: Ensure that the goals align with the overall business objectives and are relevant to the target audience.

Time-bound: Set a specific timeframe or deadline for achieving the goals to create a sense of urgency and accountability.

Consideration of Target Audience:
When defining advertising goals, it is important to consider the needs, preferences, and behaviors of the target audience. Understanding the target audience demographics, interests, and motivations allows businesses to set goals that are relevant and meaningful to their intended audience. For example, if the target audience is primarily active on Instagram, setting a goal to increase engagement on that platform would be more effective than focusing on a platform that the audience does not frequently use.

Flexibility for Optimization:
Advertising goals should allow for flexibility and optimization throughout the campaign. As the campaign progresses, it is essential to monitor performance metrics and make data-driven adjustments to improve results.

Having specific goals and regular performance tracking enables businesses to identify areas for optimization and make necessary changes to achieve better outcomes.

Aligning Your Goals with Social Media Advertising Capabilities

When setting goals for social media advertising, it is crucial to align them with the capabilities and features offered by social media platforms. Each platform has unique characteristics and advertising options that can impact the feasibility and success of specific goals. By understanding these capabilities and aligning goals accordingly, businesses can optimize their advertising strategies and achieve better results. In this section, we will explore the importance of aligning goals with social media advertising capabilities and provide insights on how to do so effectively.

Platform-Specific Objectives:
Different social media platforms have distinct strengths and features that cater to specific advertising objectives. For example, if the goal is to increase brand awareness, platforms like Facebook, Instagram, and YouTube offer extensive reach and engagement opportunities. On the other hand, if the objective is lead generation or B2B networking, platforms like LinkedIn and Twitter may be more suitable due to their professional networking focus. By understanding the strengths and limitations of each platform, businesses can align their goals with the platforms that best serve their specific advertising objectives.

Ad Format and Creative Options: Social media platforms offer various ad formats and creative options to engage with users effectively. For example, Facebook and Instagram provide carousel ads for showcasing multiple products, while YouTube specializes in video ads. Aligning goals with ad formats and creative options allows businesses to leverage the unique strengths of each platform and create compelling ads that resonate with their target audience. Consider the nature of the business, the type of content to be promoted, and the preferences of the target audience when selecting ad formats and creative elements.

Targeting Capabilities: Social media platforms provide robust targeting capabilities that allow businesses to reach specific audiences based on demographics, interests, behaviors, and more. Aligning goals with targeting capabilities ensures that advertising efforts are directed towards the most relevant audience. For example, if the goal is to target professionals in a specific industry, LinkedIn's targeting options can be utilized to reach the desired audience effectively. By understanding the targeting capabilities of each platform, businesses can align their goals with the platforms that offer the most precise and effective targeting options.

Performance Tracking and Analytics: Social media platforms provide comprehensive analytics and tracking tools that allow businesses to measure the performance of their advertising campaigns. By aligning goals with the available performance tracking and analytics features, businesses can effectively monitor the progress of their campaigns and make data-driven decisions. For instance, if the goal is to track website conversions, platforms like Facebook and Google Ads provide conversion tracking tools that enable businesses to measure the effectiveness of their ads in driving desired actions.

Budget and Cost Considerations: Aligning goals with budget and cost considerations is essential for optimizing advertising strategies. Different social media platforms offer various pricing models and bidding strategies, which can impact the budget allocation and cost per result. Understanding the cost structures of each platform and aligning goals with budgetary considerations ensures that advertising goals are realistic and achievable within the allocated resources.

SMART Goal Setting for Effective Campaigns

Setting SMART goals is a proven approach for creating effective social media advertising campaigns. The SMART framework ensures that goals are specific, measurable, achievable, relevant, and time-bound, providing businesses with a clear roadmap and measurable targets to work towards. By following this framework, businesses can increase the likelihood of campaign success and track progress effectively. In this section, we will delve into each element of SMART goal setting and explain its importance in creating effective campaigns.

Specific: A specific goal clearly defines what needs to be accomplished. It avoids vague statements and provides a precise direction for the advertising campaign.

For example, instead of setting a general goal like "increase brand awareness," a specific goal would be "increase brand awareness by 20% among the target audience within three months." Specific goals enable businesses to focus their efforts and develop tailored strategies to achieve the desired outcome.

Measurable: Measuring progress and success is essential in determining the effectiveness of an advertising campaign. Measurable goals involve establishing concrete metrics and key performance indicators (KPIs) that can be tracked and analyzed. For instance, if the goal is to drive website traffic, a measurable metric would be the number of website visits generated through social media ads. Measurable goals provide businesses with quantifiable data to evaluate campaign performance and make data-driven decisions for optimization.

Achievable: Goals should be realistic and attainable within the available resources, capabilities, and timeframe. Setting unattainable goals can lead to frustration and demotivation. Assessing the resources, budget, team capacity, and market conditions is crucial in determining what can be realistically achieved. While it is important to aim high, setting achievable goals ensures that efforts are focused on meaningful outcomes that can be accomplished.

Relevant: Goals should be relevant and aligned with the overall business objectives and marketing strategy. They should have a direct impact on the success of the business and contribute to its growth. Aligning goals with the broader objectives ensures that advertising efforts are purposeful and contribute to the overall business strategy.

For example, if the business objective is to increase sales, setting a relevant goal would be to generate a specific number of qualified leads through social media advertising.

Time-bound: Goals need to have a specific timeframe or deadline for completion. Setting a timeline creates a sense of urgency, accountability, and helps in prioritizing tasks. It also allows for the measurement of progress and the evaluation of campaign success. For example, a time-bound goal could be to achieve a 10% increase in social media engagement within one month. Setting deadlines ensures that campaigns stay on track and enables businesses to assess their performance within a defined period.

By setting SMART goals, businesses can increase their chances of campaign success. SMART goal setting provides clarity, measurement, achievability, relevance, and a sense of urgency, which are essential components of effective campaigns. It helps businesses stay focused, evaluate progress, optimize strategies, and achieve meaningful outcomes. When combined with thorough planning, strategic execution, and continuous monitoring, SMART goals serve as a guide for creating impactful social media advertising campaigns.

Understanding Your Target Audience Demographics

Understanding the demographics of your target audience is a crucial aspect of effective social media advertising. Demographics refer to the characteristics and attributes of a specific group of people, such as age, gender, location, income, education, occupation, and more. By gaining a deep understanding of your target audience's demographics, businesses can create targeted and personalized advertising campaigns that resonate with their intended audience. In this section, we will explore the importance of understanding target audience demographics and provide insights on how to do so effectively.

Targeted Messaging: Understanding target audience demographics allows businesses to tailor their messaging to resonate with specific groups. Different demographic segments have unique preferences, interests, and motivations. For example, if your target audience consists of younger individuals, you may need to adopt a more casual and relatable tone in your messaging. By aligning the content, language, and tone of your advertising with the demographics of your audience, you can increase the likelihood of capturing their attention and engaging them effectively.

Precise Targeting: Demographic information helps in precise audience targeting on social media platforms. Most social media platforms offer advanced targeting capabilities that allow businesses to reach specific demographics based on factors such as age, gender, location, and interests.

By understanding the demographic composition of your target audience, you can leverage these targeting options to ensure your ads are seen by the right people. Precise targeting not only enhances the effectiveness of your campaigns but also optimizes your advertising budget by reaching those most likely to be interested in your products or services.

Personalization and Relevance: Demographic insights enable businesses to personalize their advertising efforts. By understanding the specific characteristics and preferences of your target audience, you can create customized content and offers that are relevant to their needs. For example, if your target audience is predominantly located in a specific region, you can tailor your ads to highlight location-specific benefits or promotions.

Personalization increases the relevance of your advertising, making it more likely to resonate with your audience and drive engagement.

Market Segmentation: Demographic information forms the basis for market segmentation, which involves dividing a broader target audience into smaller, more homogeneous groups. By segmenting your target audience based on demographics, you can identify distinct customer segments with shared characteristics and behaviors. This allows for the development of targeted marketing strategies and tailored messaging for each segment. Market segmentation helps businesses understand the unique needs of different demographic groups and design advertising campaigns that address those specific needs effectively.

Data-Driven Decision Making: Understanding target audience demographics provides businesses with valuable data for making informed decisions. By analyzing demographic information, businesses can identify trends, patterns, and opportunities within their target audience. This data can guide the development of advertising strategies, content creation, and campaign optimization. By leveraging data-driven insights, businesses can refine their targeting, messaging, and overall approach to social media advertising.

Conducting Market Research for Audience Insights

Market research plays a vital role in understanding the preferences, needs, and behaviors of your target audience. By conducting thorough market research, businesses can gather valuable insights that inform their social media advertising strategies. This research provides a deeper understanding of consumer motivations, helps identify trends, and guides decision-making to create more effective campaigns. In this section, we will explore the importance of conducting market research for audience insights and provide insights on how to do so effectively.

Identify Target Audience: Market research helps identify and define the specific target audience for your social media advertising campaigns. It involves gathering information about demographics, psychographics, and consumer characteristics that align with your business objectives. Understanding who your target audience is allows you to create more tailored and relevant advertising messages, increasing the likelihood of engaging your desired audience.

Consumer Behavior Analysis: Market research provides insights into consumer behavior, including purchasing patterns, decision-making processes, and engagement preferences. By analyzing consumer behavior, you can gain a deeper understanding of how your target audience interacts with social media platforms, what motivates their purchasing decisions, and which types of content they find most appealing. This knowledge allows you to design campaigns that align with consumer preferences and effectively influence their decision-making.

Competitor Analysis: Market research also involves analyzing your competitors' strategies and tactics. By studying the competition, you can identify gaps, opportunities, and areas for differentiation in the market. Understanding how your competitors are engaging with their audience on social media platforms can provide valuable insights for developing your own unique advertising approach. By leveraging competitor analysis, you can identify best practices, learn from their successes and failures, and tailor your advertising strategies accordingly.

Surveys and Questionnaires: Surveys and questionnaires are valuable tools for gathering direct insights from your target audience. You can create online surveys or questionnaires to gather feedback on preferences, perceptions, and opinions related to your industry, products, or services.

These tools enable you to collect quantitative and qualitative data that can be used to inform your advertising strategies and campaign development.

Social Listening: Social listening involves monitoring conversations and discussions happening on social media platforms related to your industry, brand, or products. By monitoring social media channels, hashtags, and keywords, you can gain real-time insights into the opinions, sentiments, and trends that are relevant to your target audience. Social listening allows you to tap into the collective voice of your audience, identify their pain points, and understand their needs, which can then be addressed through your advertising campaigns.

Data Analytics: Utilizing data analytics tools provided by social media platforms and other sources allows you to gain insights into user behavior, engagement metrics, and campaign performance. By analyzing data, you can identify patterns, trends, and areas for improvement. Data analytics enables you to make data-driven decisions, optimize your advertising strategies, and measure the effectiveness of your campaigns.

Utilizing Social Media Analytics and Tools for Audience Segmentation

Social media platforms provide a wealth of data and analytics that can be leveraged to gain insights into your target audience. By effectively utilizing social media analytics and tools, businesses can segment their audience based on various characteristics and behaviors.

Audience segmentation allows for more targeted and personalized advertising campaigns, leading to higher engagement and better results. In this section, we will explore the importance of utilizing social media analytics and tools for audience segmentation and provide insights on how to do so effectively.

Demographic Segmentation: Social media platforms offer demographic data about your audience, including age, gender, location, and language. This information is valuable for segmenting your audience based on these factors. By understanding the demographic composition of your audience, you can tailor your advertising messages to resonate with specific groups and optimize your targeting strategies.

Psychographic Segmentation: Psychographic segmentation involves understanding the psychological characteristics, interests, and behaviors of your audience. Social media analytics provide insights into the interests, hobbies, pages liked, and activities of your audience. By analyzing these psychographic data points, you can create segments based on shared interests or preferences, allowing for more targeted advertising that aligns with your audience's passions and motivations.

Behavioral Segmentation: Social media platforms track user behavior, such as engagement with posts, frequency of visits, and interactions with ads. This behavioral data helps segment your audience based on their level of engagement, purchase history, and other actions taken on your social media profiles.

By segmenting your audience based on behavioral attributes, you can deliver more personalized and relevant advertising messages, increasing the likelihood of conversion.

Lookalike Audiences: Social media platforms offer a powerful feature known as lookalike audiences. Lookalike audiences are segments of users who share similar characteristics and behaviors with your existing audience or customer base. By utilizing social media analytics, you can identify the characteristics and behaviors of your most valuable customers and create lookalike audiences to expand your reach and target new potential customers who exhibit similar traits.

Custom Audience Segmentation: Social media platforms allow businesses to create custom audiences based on specific criteria. You can segment your audience based on factors like website visitors, email subscribers, or customer lists. By leveraging these custom audience segments, you can deliver tailored advertising messages to specific groups, enhancing the relevance and effectiveness of your campaigns.

A/B Testing: Social media analytics also enable businesses to conduct A/B testing to optimize their advertising campaigns. A/B testing involves creating multiple variations of ads or targeting strategies and measuring their performance. By analyzing the data provided by social media analytics, you can identify which variations are resonating best with different segments of your audience. This allows you to refine your targeting, messaging, and creative elements to maximize engagement and conversion rates.

By utilizing social media analytics and tools for audience segmentation, businesses can create more targeted and effective advertising campaigns. Understanding the demographic, psychographic, and behavioral attributes of your audience allows for personalized messaging, precise targeting, and optimized campaign strategies. Social media analytics enable businesses to make data-driven decisions, refine their advertising approach, and achieve better results. By leveraging these tools, businesses can connect with their audience on a deeper level, increase engagement, and drive meaningful actions.

The Importance of Engaging Ad Content

In the world of social media advertising, where users are constantly bombarded with an abundance of content, capturing and maintaining the attention of your audience is paramount. Engaging ad content plays a crucial role in cutting through the noise and capturing the interest of your target audience. In this section, we will explore the importance of engaging ad content and discuss why it is essential for the success of your social media advertising campaigns.

Capturing Attention: Engaging ad content is instrumental in capturing the attention of your audience amidst the sea of content they encounter daily. Social media platforms are highly competitive spaces, and users have limited attention spans.

Your ad content needs to be compelling and attention-grabbing from the moment it appears on their screens. Whether it's a captivating headline, an eye-catching visual, or a thought-provoking question, engaging content creates an immediate connection and entices users to pay attention.

Increasing Brand Recall: Engaging ad content has the power to leave a lasting impression on your audience. When your ads resonate with users and evoke positive emotions or experiences, they are more likely to remember your brand. Memorable content helps build brand recall, ensuring that when users are ready to make a purchasing decision or need the products or services you offer, they think of your brand first. By creating engaging ad content, you can increase brand awareness and establish a stronger presence in the minds of your audience.

Driving Engagement and Interactions: Engaging ad content encourages users to take action and interact with your brand. Whether it's liking, commenting, sharing, or clicking through to your website, compelling content motivates users to engage with your ads. Increased engagement not only expands the reach of your ads but also fosters a sense of community and connection with your audience. When users feel compelled to interact with your content, it opens doors for deeper engagement, brand loyalty, and potential conversions.

Building Trust and Credibility: Engaging ad content helps build trust and credibility with your audience. When your content is valuable, informative, or entertaining, it positions your brand as an authority in your industry. It demonstrates that you understand your audience's needs and can provide solutions or experiences that resonate with them.

Engaging content showcases your brand's expertise, fosters trust, and encourages users to view your brand as a reliable source.

Encouraging Virality and Word-of-Mouth: Engaging ad content has the potential to go viral, spreading across social media platforms and reaching a wider audience. When users find content that resonates with them, they are more likely to share it with their own networks, amplifying its reach and generating word-of-mouth promotion for your brand. Viral content has the power to exponentially increase brand exposure, attract new customers, and enhance brand reputation.

Enhancing Ad Performance: Engaging ad content directly impacts the performance of your advertising campaigns. When users find your content compelling and relevant, they are more likely to engage with it, spend more time interacting with your ads, and take desired actions such as clicking through to your website or making a purchase. Social media platforms also reward engaging content by prioritizing it in users' feeds, leading to increased visibility and reach for your ads.

Best Practices for Writing Compelling Ad Copy

Crafting compelling ad copy is a vital aspect of creating successful social media advertising campaigns. The words you use in your ads have the power to capture attention, convey your brand message, and persuade your audience to take action. In this section, we will explore some best practices for writing compelling ad copy that resonates with your target audience and drives results.

Know Your Audience: Understanding your target audience is crucial for writing compelling ad copy. Research their demographics, interests, pain points, and motivations to tailor your messaging accordingly. Use language and tone that resonates with your audience and speaks directly to their needs, desires, and aspirations.

Keep it Concise: In the fast-paced world of social media, attention spans are short. Keep your ad copy concise and to the point. Use clear and concise language that effectively communicates your message without unnecessary fluff. Focus on the most impactful and relevant information to grab attention and maintain engagement.

Highlight Benefits: Instead of simply listing features, emphasize the benefits of your product or service in your ad copy. Help your audience understand how your offering solves their problems or improves their lives. Highlight the value they will gain by engaging with your brand, and explain how it will make a positive difference for them.

Create a Sense of Urgency: Incorporate elements of urgency and scarcity into your ad copy to prompt immediate action. Use phrases like "limited time offer," "exclusive deal," or "act now" to create a sense of urgency and encourage your audience to take action promptly. By instilling a fear of missing out (FOMO), you can drive conversions and increase engagement.

Use Power Words: Power words are impactful and emotionally charged words that evoke a strong response from your audience.

Incorporate words that convey emotions, such as "amazing," "exciting," "exclusive," "transformative," or "unforgettable." These words can create a sense of intrigue and excitement, enticing your audience to learn more about your brand.

Incorporate a Strong Call-to-Action (CTA): Every compelling ad copy should include a clear and compelling call-to-action. The CTA tells your audience what action to take, whether it's "Shop Now," "Sign Up Today," "Learn More," or "Book Now." Make sure your CTA is prominent, visually appealing, and creates a sense of urgency or value for your audience.

Test and Iterate: Don't settle for one version of your ad copy. Test different variations to see what resonates best with your audience. Experiment with different headlines, descriptions, or language choices.

Analyze the performance metrics and iterate based on the results to optimize your ad copy for maximum impact.

Be Authentic and Unique: Stand out from the competition by being authentic and unique in your ad copy. Avoid using generic or clichéd language that blends in with other ads. Find your brand voice and use it consistently across your ad copy to create a distinctive identity that resonates with your audience.

Use Social Proof: Incorporate social proof elements in your ad copy to build credibility and trust. Highlight customer testimonials, ratings, reviews, or user-generated content that demonstrates the positive experiences others have had with your brand. Social proof can reinforce the value of your offering and persuade your audience to engage with your brand.

Edit and Proofread: Before launching your ad, make sure to edit and proofread your copy. Ensure that it is free from grammatical errors, typos, or confusing language. A well-polished ad copy reflects professionalism and enhances the credibility of your brand.

Choosing Captivating Visuals for Your Ads

Visual content plays a vital role in capturing the attention of your audience and conveying your brand message effectively. When it comes to social media advertising, selecting captivating visuals is essential for creating eye-catching and memorable ads.

In this section, we will explore the importance of choosing captivating visuals for your ads and provide some best practices to help you make the right choices.

Grab Attention: The primary purpose of captivating visuals is to grab the attention of your audience as they scroll through their social media feeds. Choose images or videos that are visually striking, bold, and unique. Use vibrant colors, high-quality graphics, or visually stunning compositions that stand out from the crowd. Captivating visuals will make users pause and take notice of your ad amidst the sea of content.

Reflect Your Brand Identity: The visuals you select should align with your brand identity and communicate your brand's personality and values. Consider your brand's aesthetics, color palette, and overall style when choosing visuals for your ads. Consistency in visual branding helps create a cohesive and recognizable presence for your brand across different platforms.

Tell a Story: Visuals have the power to tell stories and evoke emotions. Choose images or videos that convey a narrative or evoke a specific feeling relevant to your brand or product. Storytelling visuals capture the imagination of your audience and create a deeper connection with your brand. Whether it's showcasing a customer's journey, illustrating a problem and its solution, or highlighting the experience your product offers, tell a compelling story through your visuals.

Showcase Your Product or Service: If your goal is to promote a specific product or service, make sure your visuals effectively showcase it. Highlight the unique features, benefits, or uses of your offering through compelling visuals.

Show your product in action or demonstrate how it solves a problem for your audience. Use close-ups, angles, or dynamic compositions to create intrigue and highlight key aspects of your product.

Use Authentic and Relatable Imagery: Authenticity and relatability are crucial in connecting with your audience. Choose visuals that feature real people, genuine expressions, and authentic moments. Use imagery that reflects the diversity and experiences of your target audience. Authentic visuals help build trust, as they resonate with users and create a sense of familiarity and relevance.

Consider Mobile Optimization: As a significant portion of social media users access platforms on mobile devices, it is essential to optimize your visuals for mobile viewing. Select visuals that are clear, easily recognizable, and visually appealing even on smaller screens. Avoid using complex or cluttered visuals that may become difficult to understand or appreciate on mobile devices.

Test Different Visual Variations: Just as with ad copy, it's essential to test different visual variations to see what resonates best with your audience. Experiment with different images, videos, or graphics to determine which ones generate the highest engagement and conversion rates. Analyze the performance metrics and iterate based on the results to optimize your visual choices for maximum impact.

Maintain Consistency Across Platforms: When running ad campaigns on multiple social media platforms, maintain consistency in your visual branding. While adapting your visuals to suit each platform's specifications, ensure that there is a cohesive look and feel across all ads. Consistency in visuals helps build brand recognition and reinforces your messaging regardless of the platform users are on.

Complement Visuals with Compelling Copy: While visuals are crucial, they should work hand in hand with compelling ad copy. Ensure that your visuals and copy complement each other and convey a consistent message. The combination of captivating visuals and persuasive copy creates a powerful impact and enhances the overall effectiveness of your ads.

Evaluating Popular Social Media Platforms for Advertising

When it comes to social media advertising, selecting the right platforms to reach your target audience is crucial for the success of your campaigns. With numerous social media platforms available, it's essential to evaluate them based on various factors to determine which ones align with your advertising goals and audience demographics. In this section, we will explore the process of evaluating popular social media platforms for advertising and discuss key considerations to help you make informed decisions.

User Demographics: Start by understanding the user demographics of each social media platform. Analyze data and research to identify which platforms attract the largest percentage of your target audience.

Consider factors such as age, gender, location, interests, and behavior to ensure that your chosen platforms align with the demographics of your ideal customers.

Platform Reach and Usage: Assess the reach and usage of each social media platform to determine its potential impact on your advertising efforts. Look for platforms with a significant number of active users and high engagement rates. Evaluate factors such as the number of monthly active users, daily active users, and average time spent on the platform per session. Platforms with a large and engaged user base offer more opportunities to reach and connect with your target audience.

Ad Formats and Features: Examine the ad formats and features offered by each social media platform. Consider the types of ads you can create, such as image ads, video ads, carousel ads, or stories ads. Evaluate whether the platform provides advanced targeting options, retargeting capabilities, or interactive ad features. Assess how these ad formats and features align with your advertising goals and the type of content that resonates with your audience.

Audience Engagement and Interactions: Look into the level of audience engagement and interactions on each platform. Evaluate the platform's engagement metrics, such as likes, comments, shares, and click-through rates. Consider whether the platform fosters meaningful interactions and encourages users to engage with brands. Platforms with higher engagement rates offer better opportunities for brand awareness, customer interaction, and potential conversions.

Content Suitability: Assess whether the nature of the content on each platform aligns with your brand and advertising objectives. Different platforms cater to different types of content, such as visual imagery, short-form text, long-form articles, or video content. Consider whether the platform's content format and style resonate with your brand's voice and messaging. Ensure that your chosen platforms can accommodate the type of content that best represents your brand and engages your target audience.

Platform Advertising Costs: Evaluate the cost of advertising on each platform. Consider factors such as ad pricing models (e.g., cost-per-click, cost-per-impression), average ad costs, and the level of competition among advertisers. Compare the cost-effectiveness of each platform based on your budget and expected return on investment (ROI).

Keep in mind that platforms with higher ad costs may also offer better targeting options and reach.

Analytics and Measurement: Look into the analytics and measurement capabilities provided by each platform. Consider whether the platform offers robust analytics tools to track and measure the performance of your ads. Evaluate whether you can access important metrics such as impressions, reach, engagement, click-through rates, and conversions. Effective analytics and measurement capabilities enable you to optimize your campaigns, make data-driven decisions, and maximize the impact of your advertising efforts.

Brand Fit and Platform Reputation: Lastly, consider the brand fit and reputation of each social media platform. Evaluate whether the platform aligns with your brand values and image. Consider the platform's reputation, user sentiment, and any controversies or issues associated with it. Choose platforms that resonate with your brand's identity and maintain a positive image that aligns with your target audience's expectations.

By thoroughly evaluating popular social media platforms based on these factors, you can make informed decisions about where to allocate your advertising efforts and resources. Remember that a multi-platform approach may be beneficial, depending on your target audience's behavior and preferences. Regularly monitor the performance of your campaigns, analyze data, and make adjustments to optimize your advertising strategy for maximum impact.

Understanding Platform Demographics and User Behavior

When it comes to social media advertising, understanding the demographics and user behavior on different platforms is crucial for effectively reaching and engaging your target audience. Each social media platform attracts a unique set of users with distinct characteristics and preferences. In this section, we will explore the importance of understanding platform demographics and user behavior and how it can inform your advertising strategies.

Demographic Insights: Start by gathering demographic insights about the users on each social media platform. Analyze data and research to identify the age groups, gender distribution, locations, and other relevant demographic information of the platform's user base.

Understanding the demographics of each platform helps you determine whether it aligns with your target audience and if it provides an opportunity to reach the right people.

User Behavior and Preferences: In addition to demographics, understanding user behavior and preferences on different platforms is crucial. Analyze how users interact with content, engage with brands, and make purchasing decisions on each platform. Look into factors such as the types of content they prefer (e.g., images, videos, articles), the frequency of their interactions, and the level of engagement they exhibit. This information helps you tailor your content and advertising approach to meet user expectations and preferences.

Platform-Specific Features: Each social media platform offers unique features that influence user behavior and engagement.

For example, Instagram is known for its visually appealing imagery, while Twitter focuses on concise and real-time updates. Explore the platform-specific features such as stories, live videos, hashtags, or groups and understand how users utilize them. By leveraging these features effectively, you can align your advertising strategies with the platform's user behavior and maximize engagement.

Timing and Frequency: Consider the timing and frequency of user activity on each platform. Determine when users are most active and likely to engage with content. Some platforms may have peak usage times during specific days or hours. By understanding these patterns, you can schedule your posts and advertisements to reach users when they are most receptive, increasing the likelihood of engagement and conversion.

Social Interactions and Influencer Culture: Social media platforms thrive on social interactions and the influence of content creators or influencers. Analyze how users interact with each other, share content, and respond to influencer endorsements. Identify influential users within your target audience and explore opportunities for collaborations or partnerships. Understanding the dynamics of social interactions and the role of influencers on each platform allows you to leverage these relationships for your advertising campaigns.

User Privacy and Data Regulations: Stay informed about the privacy policies and data regulations specific to each platform. Understand how user data is collected, stored, and utilized by the platform and its advertisers. Ensure that your advertising strategies comply with privacy regulations and respect user preferences regarding data usage.

By prioritizing user privacy and data protection, you can build trust with your audience and maintain a positive brand image.

Feedback and Reviews: Pay attention to user feedback and reviews on each platform. Monitor comments, ratings, and reviews related to your brand or industry. This feedback provides valuable insights into user sentiment, preferences, and pain points. It helps you understand how users perceive your brand and identify areas for improvement. Incorporate user feedback into your advertising strategies to enhance the relevance and effectiveness of your campaigns.

By understanding the demographics and user behavior on different social media platforms, you can tailor your advertising strategies to effectively engage your target audience.

Remember to regularly monitor and adapt your strategies based on user behavior changes and platform updates to ensure the continued success of your social media advertising campaigns.

Choosing the Platforms that Align with Your Target Audience and Goals

When it comes to social media advertising, selecting the right platforms that align with your target audience and goals is crucial for maximizing the effectiveness of your campaigns. With numerous platforms available, it's essential to identify the platforms where your target audience is most active and where your advertising objectives can be best achieved.

In this section, we will explore the importance of choosing platforms that align with your target audience and goals and provide some key considerations to help you make informed decisions.

Understand Your Target Audience: Begin by gaining a deep understanding of your target audience. Analyze their demographics, interests, behaviors, and preferences. Consider factors such as age, gender, location, profession, hobbies, and lifestyle. By having a clear picture of your target audience, you can identify the social media platforms they are most likely to use and engage with.

Research Platform Demographics: Research and analyze the demographics of different social media platforms. Look for data on the user base, including age range, gender distribution, and geographical location.

Compare these demographics with your target audience profile to identify the platforms that closely match your audience's characteristics. Choose platforms where a significant portion of your target audience is actively present.

Platform Usage and Behavior: Evaluate the usage patterns and behaviors of your target audience on different platforms. Consider factors such as how frequently they visit the platform, the time they spend on it, and the activities they engage in (e.g., content consumption, interaction with brands, sharing content). Align your advertising goals with platforms that best facilitate the desired user behavior and provide opportunities for engagement.

Consider Platform Relevance: Assess the relevance of each platform to your industry and the nature of your business.

Some platforms may be more suitable for certain industries or types of products/services. For example, visually-oriented platforms like Instagram or Pinterest are ideal for businesses with highly visual products or services. Consider the content format, style, and communication norms of each platform to determine if it aligns with your brand and messaging.

Evaluate Advertising Features: Explore the advertising features and capabilities offered by each platform. Consider the types of ad formats available, targeting options, and tracking capabilities. Evaluate whether the platform provides the tools and features necessary to achieve your advertising goals. For instance, if your objective is to drive website traffic, platforms with robust link-sharing and click-through tracking features may be more suitable.

Analyze Competitor Presence:
Research your competitors' presence on different social media platforms. Identify the platforms where they have a strong presence and analyze their strategies and engagement levels. This analysis can provide valuable insights into which platforms are effective within your industry and give you an idea of where your target audience is likely to be active.

Set Clear Advertising Goals: Define your advertising goals and objectives clearly. Consider whether you aim to increase brand awareness, drive website traffic, generate leads, boost sales, or engage with your audience. Different platforms may be better suited for specific goals. For example, if your goal is to engage with your audience and build a community, platforms with strong community-building features like Facebook Groups may be a good fit.

Test and Iterate: Remember that social media platforms are constantly evolving, and user behavior may change over time. It's important to test different platforms and evaluate their performance. Start with a few platforms that align with your audience and goals, monitor the results, and make data-driven decisions. Continuously optimize your advertising strategy by allocating resources to the platforms that generate the best outcomes.

Setting Advertising Budgets for Different Platforms

Setting advertising budgets for different social media platforms is a crucial aspect of planning your advertising campaigns effectively. Allocating the right budget to each platform ensures that you can reach your target audience, maximize your ad visibility, and achieve your advertising goals. In this section, we will explore the key considerations when setting advertising budgets for different platforms.

Define Your Overall Advertising Budget: Start by determining your overall advertising budget. Consider your business objectives, revenue goals, and the resources available for marketing activities. Setting a clear budget helps you allocate funds strategically across different platforms and campaigns.

Research Platform Advertising Costs: Conduct research to understand the advertising costs associated with each social media platform. Different platforms may have varying pricing models, such as cost-per-click (CPC), cost-per-impression (CPM), or cost-per-action (CPA). Evaluate the average costs per ad and the potential reach you can achieve within your budget constraints.

Consider Platform Popularity and Reach: Take into account the popularity and reach of each platform when allocating your budget. Platforms with a larger user base and higher engagement rates may require a higher budget to reach a significant portion of your target audience. Consider the potential return on investment (ROI) based on the platform's reach and the value you can derive from reaching a larger audience.

Analyze Platform Performance and Historical Data: Review the performance of your previous campaigns on different platforms if available. Analyze the metrics and data to identify which platforms have generated the highest engagement, conversions, or ROI. Use this information to allocate a larger portion of your budget to platforms that have historically performed well for your business.

Align Budgets with Campaign Objectives: Consider your campaign objectives when setting budgets for different platforms. For example, if your objective is to drive brand awareness, you may allocate a higher budget to platforms that excel at reaching a broad audience and generating impressions. If your goal is lead generation, you may focus more on platforms that offer advanced targeting capabilities and lead generation features.

Test and Optimize Budget Allocation: When starting a new campaign or exploring new platforms, it is advisable to allocate a smaller portion of your budget for initial testing and optimization. This allows you to assess the performance of different platforms and make data-driven decisions. Once you gather insights and determine the platforms that deliver the desired results, you can adjust your budget allocation accordingly.

Consider Ad Format and Competition: The ad format you choose and the level of competition on each platform can also influence budget allocation. Platforms with highly engaging ad formats or those with intense competition may require a higher budget to stand out and achieve your desired outcomes. Evaluate the ad formats, placements, and the potential impact they can have on your campaign performance.

Monitor and Adjust: It's important to continuously monitor the performance of your campaigns and adjust your budgets as needed. Analyze key performance metrics such as click-through rates, conversion rates, cost per acquisition, and return on ad spend. If you find that certain platforms are consistently underperforming or not delivering the expected results, consider reallocating your budget to more effective platforms.

Remember that setting advertising budgets for different platforms is an ongoing process. Regularly review and optimize your budget allocation based on the performance of your campaigns, changes in platform dynamics, and shifts in your business goals. By carefully allocating your budget to the most relevant platforms, you can maximize the impact of your advertising efforts and achieve a higher return on investment.

Understanding Bidding Strategies and Optimization Techniques

In social media advertising, bidding strategies and optimization techniques play a crucial role in maximizing the effectiveness of your campaigns and ensuring optimal use of your advertising budget. Bidding strategies determine how you bid for ad placements, while optimization techniques help you refine your campaigns based on performance data. In this section, we will explore the importance of understanding bidding strategies and optimization techniques and provide an overview of some commonly used approaches.

Cost Models: Social media platforms typically offer different cost models for bidding, such as cost-per-click (CPC), cost-per-impression (CPM), or cost-per-action (CPA). Understand the cost model options available on each platform and choose the one that aligns with your campaign objectives and key performance indicators (KPIs). For example, if your goal is to drive website traffic, CPC bidding may be more suitable.

Manual Bidding: Manual bidding allows you to have full control over how much you are willing to bid for ad placements. You set a maximum bid, and the platform will aim to deliver your ads while trying to maximize your results within your specified bid range. Manual bidding is ideal if you want to have precise control over your budget and bid amounts.

Automatic Bidding: Automatic bidding, also known as algorithmic bidding or automated bidding, leverages the platform's algorithms to automatically optimize your bids based on your campaign objectives. The platform uses machine learning and historical performance data to adjust bids in real-time, aiming to achieve the best results for your given budget. Automatic bidding can be a time-saving option and is recommended for advertisers who may not have the expertise or time to manually adjust bids.

Targeting and Bid Adjustments: Social media platforms offer various targeting options, such as demographic targeting, interest-based targeting, or remarketing. These targeting options allow you to refine your audience and adjust your bids accordingly. For example, you can increase bids for a specific demographic that has shown higher engagement or adjust bids for users who have previously interacted with your website. Use targeting and bid adjustments to focus your budget on the most relevant audience segments.

Ad Placement Optimization: Different ad placements on social media platforms can have varying levels of performance and costs. It's essential to analyze the performance of your ads across different placements and optimize your bidding strategy accordingly. Allocate more budget to placements that generate higher engagement, conversions, or better ROI. Experiment with different placements to find the most effective ones for your campaign objectives.

Ad Scheduling and Dayparting: Consider the time of day or days of the week when your target audience is most active on social media platforms. Some platforms allow you to schedule your ads or adjust bids based on specific times or days. By understanding the behavior of your audience and their engagement patterns, you can optimize your bidding strategy to focus on peak activity periods and allocate budget accordingly.

Conversion Tracking and Optimization: Implement conversion tracking to measure the performance of your ads and optimize your bidding strategy based on actual conversions. By tracking conversions, you can identify which ads, targeting options, or placements are driving the desired actions. Adjust your bids accordingly to maximize the return on your advertising investment.

A/B Testing and Iterative Optimization: Conduct A/B tests to compare different ad variations, targeting options, or bidding strategies. Test different elements such as ad copy, visuals, audience segments, or bidding approaches to identify the most effective combinations. Use the insights gained from A/B tests to refine your bidding strategy and optimize your campaigns iteratively.

Monitoring and Performance Analysis: Continuously monitor the performance of your campaigns and analyze key performance metrics such as click-through rates, conversion rates, cost per acquisition, or return on ad spend. Identify underperforming ads, placements, or targeting options and make data-driven decisions to adjust your bidding strategy. Regularly review performance data to identify trends, patterns, and areas for improvement.

Platform-Specific Optimization Tools: Social media platforms often provide optimization tools and recommendations to help improve your campaign performance. Utilize these tools to get insights, suggestions, and optimization recommendations tailored to each platform. Experiment with different settings and options provided by the platforms to maximize the effectiveness of your bidding strategy.

Understanding bidding strategies and optimization techniques is essential for achieving your advertising goals and maximizing the results of your social media campaigns. By choosing the right bidding approach, leveraging targeting and bid adjustments, optimizing placements and ad scheduling, tracking conversions, conducting A/B tests, and continuously monitoring performance, you can refine your bidding strategy over time and drive better outcomes from your advertising efforts.

Tips for Maximizing ROI and Minimizing Costs

When it comes to social media advertising, maximizing return on investment (ROI) and minimizing costs are key objectives for advertisers. By implementing effective strategies and making smart decisions, you can optimize your campaigns to achieve better results while keeping your expenses in check. Here are some tips to help you maximize ROI and minimize costs in your social media advertising efforts:

Set Clear and Measurable Goals: Start by defining clear and measurable goals for your campaigns. Whether it's increasing brand awareness, driving website traffic, generating leads, or boosting sales, having well-defined goals allows you to focus your efforts and allocate resources efficiently.

Know Your Target Audience: Understanding your target audience is crucial for efficient advertising. Conduct thorough research to identify their demographics, interests, behaviors, and preferences. By targeting the right audience segments, you can improve the relevance of your ads, which can lead to higher engagement and conversion rates.

Refine Your Targeting and Segmentation: Utilize the targeting and segmentation capabilities provided by social media platforms. Narrow down your audience based on factors such as location, age, gender, interests, and past interactions. The more targeted your audience, the more likely you are to reach people who are genuinely interested in your products or services, resulting in better ROI.

Leverage Lookalike Audiences: Lookalike audiences allow you to reach new users who share similar characteristics with your existing customers or engaged audience. By targeting lookalike audiences, you can expand your reach to people who are more likely to be interested in your offerings. This can lead to increased ROI by maximizing the impact of your advertising budget.

Optimize Ad Creative: Create compelling and visually appealing ad content that grabs attention and resonates with your target audience. Test different ad formats, visuals, headlines, and calls-to-action to find the combinations that generate the best results. Continuously optimize your ad creative based on performance data to improve engagement and conversion rates.

Implement Conversion Tracking: Implement conversion tracking to measure the effectiveness of your campaigns. By tracking conversions, such as purchases, sign-ups, or downloads, you can evaluate the performance of your ads and optimize your budget allocation accordingly. Focus on the campaigns, ad sets, or creatives that deliver the highest conversion rates to maximize ROI.

Monitor Key Performance Metrics: Regularly monitor key performance metrics such as click-through rates (CTR), conversion rates, cost per acquisition (CPA), and return on ad spend (ROAS). Analyze these metrics to identify trends, patterns, and areas for improvement. Optimize your campaigns based on the insights gained from performance analysis to achieve better results.

Conduct A/B Testing: A/B testing involves comparing two or more variations of your ads or targeting strategies to determine which performs better. Test different elements such as ad copy, visuals, audience segments, or bidding strategies. By conducting A/B tests, you can identify the most effective approaches and optimize your campaigns accordingly, leading to improved ROI.

Optimize Bidding Strategies: Experiment with different bidding strategies, such as manual bidding or automatic bidding, to find the approach that works best for your goals and budget. Adjust your bids based on performance data and focus on placements, audiences, or times that deliver better results. Continuously optimize your bidding strategies to maximize ROI and minimize costs.

Regularly Review and Refine: Social media advertising is an iterative process. Regularly review your campaigns, performance data, and market trends. Refine your targeting, ad creative, bidding strategies, and budget allocation based on the insights you gather. Stay updated with platform updates, new features, and best practices to optimize your campaigns continuously.

By implementing these tips, you can improve the efficiency and effectiveness of your social media advertising efforts. Maximizing ROI and minimizing costs require a combination of strategic planning, data analysis, and ongoing optimization. Keep experimenting, learning, and adapting your approach to achieve the best possible results from your social media advertising campaigns.

Chapter 7: Creating and Launching Ads

Step-by-Step Guide to Creating Ads on Various Social Media Platforms

Creating effective ads on social media platforms requires careful planning and execution. Each platform has its own ad creation process and features. In this step-by-step guide, we will walk you through the general process of creating ads on various social media platforms:

Define Your Advertising Objective: Start by clarifying your advertising objective. Are you aiming to increase brand awareness, drive website traffic, generate leads, or boost sales? Having a clear objective will guide your ad creation process.

Select the Social Media Platform: Choose the social media platform(s) that align with your target audience and advertising goals. Popular platforms include Facebook, Instagram, Twitter, LinkedIn, Pinterest, and Snapchat. Each platform has its unique user base and ad formats, so consider where your target audience is most active.

Understand the Ad Formats: Familiarize yourself with the ad formats available on your chosen platform. It could include image ads, video ads, carousel ads, story ads, or sponsored posts. Each format has different specifications, such as image dimensions, video length, and caption limits. Understanding these formats will help you create ads that meet the platform's requirements.

Set Up Your Advertising Account: Create an advertising account on the chosen social media platform.

This typically involves signing up, providing necessary information, and agreeing to the platform's advertising terms and policies. Follow the platform's instructions to set up your account.

Access the Ad Creation Interface: Once your advertising account is set up, navigate to the ad creation interface or Ads Manager on the platform. This is where you will design and configure your ads.

Define Your Target Audience: Specify the target audience for your ads. Use the platform's targeting options to select demographics, interests, behaviors, or custom audience segments. Refining your audience targeting will increase the relevance of your ads to the intended audience.

Set Your Budget and Schedule: Determine your ad budget and schedule. Set a daily or lifetime budget, and choose the start and end dates for your ad campaign. The platform will help you estimate the potential reach and frequency based on your budget settings.

Design Your Ad Creative: Create visually appealing ad creative that grabs attention and conveys your message effectively. Use captivating images, videos, or graphics that align with your brand identity. Craft compelling ad copy that entices users to take action. Tailor your creative elements to the platform's ad format requirements.

Configure Ad Placement: Select the ad placements where you want your ads to appear. This could include newsfeeds, stories, sidebars, or audience network placements. Consider the platform's best practices and recommendations for ad placement to maximize visibility and engagement.

Add Call-to-Action (CTA) and Landing Page: Include a clear and compelling call-to-action in your ad. The CTA encourages users to take the desired action, such as "Shop Now," "Learn More," or "Sign Up." Ensure that the destination URL or landing page is relevant and optimized for the user's journey.

Review and Publish: Review your ad settings, targeting, creative elements, and budget to ensure everything is accurate and aligned with your objectives. Preview the ad to see how it will appear to users. Once you're satisfied, click the "Publish" or "Submit" button to launch your ad campaign.

Monitor and Optimize: After your ads are live, monitor their performance closely. Track key metrics such as impressions, clicks, click-through rates, conversions, and cost per result.

Analyze the data to identify opportunities for optimization. Make adjustments to your targeting, creative elements, or budget as needed to improve ad performance.

A/B Testing and Iterative Optimization: Conduct A/B tests by creating variations of your ads to test different elements such as images, headlines, or CTAs. Compare the performance of each variation to determine the most effective approach. Iterate and optimize your ads based on the insights gained from the tests.

Remember, this is a general guide, and the specific steps may vary slightly depending on the social media platform you're using. It's important to familiarize yourself with the platform's ad creation interface and guidelines to ensure you make the most of their features and options.

Ad Formats, Placements, and Targeting Options

When it comes to social media advertising, understanding the available ad formats, placements, and targeting options is essential for creating effective campaigns. Each social media platform offers a range of choices to help you reach your target audience and convey your message in the most impactful way. Let's explore the key aspects of ad formats, placements, and targeting options:

Ad Formats:

Image Ads: These ads consist of a single static image with accompanying text. Image ads are widely used across social media platforms and can effectively convey your brand's message or showcase a specific product or service.

Video Ads: Video ads are engaging and allow you to tell a story or demonstrate your product in action. They can range from short snippets to longer-form videos and are an effective way to capture users' attention and communicate your message effectively.

Carousel Ads: Carousel ads enable you to showcase multiple images or videos within a single ad unit. Users can swipe through the carousel to view each image or video, providing an interactive and immersive ad experience.

Story Ads: Story ads appear in the ephemeral content format, available on platforms such as Facebook, Instagram, and Snapchat. These ads appear in users' Stories feed and offer a full-screen experience, often with vertical-oriented visuals and immersive features.

Sponsored Posts: Sponsored posts are native ads that blend seamlessly with a platform's organic content. They appear in users' feeds and mimic the style and format of regular posts, ensuring a non-intrusive advertising experience.

Ad Placements:

Newsfeed/Feed Placements: These ads appear within the main content feed of the social media platform, blending in with users' regular updates. They offer high visibility and engagement potential. **Sidebar/Column Placements**: Sidebar or column ads appear alongside the main content, usually on the desktop version of a platform. These ads are typically smaller in size but can still attract user attention. **Story Placements**: Story ads appear in the Stories section of social media platforms. They are full-screen ads that users can view by swiping through their friends' or followed accounts' Stories.

Story placements provide a more immersive and visually appealing ad experience.

Audience Network Placements: Some platforms offer the option to extend your ads beyond the platform itself and display them on a network of partner websites or apps. This broadens your reach and can help increase brand visibility.

Targeting Options:

Demographics: Target users based on age, gender, location, language, education, or other demographic factors. This allows you to tailor your ads to specific segments of your target audience.

Interests and Behaviors: Social media platforms collect data on users' interests, hobbies, and online behaviors. Leverage this information to target users who are likely to be interested in your products or services.

Custom Audiences: Upload your own customer data, such as email addresses or phone numbers, to create custom audience segments. This enables you to target existing customers or create lookalike audiences with similar characteristics.

Remarketing: Show ads to users who have interacted with your website, app, or specific content. Remarketing allows you to re-engage with users who have shown interest in your brand or products but may not have converted yet.

Lookalike Audiences: Platforms enable you to reach new users who share similar traits or characteristics with your existing customers or engaged audience. Lookalike audiences help expand your reach to potential customers who are more likely to be interested in your offerings.

Understanding the available ad formats, placements, and targeting options on social media platforms empowers you to create highly targeted and engaging campaigns. Experiment with different combinations and continuously analyze performance data to optimize your advertising efforts and achieve your goals effectively.

Best Practices for Ad Design and Creative Optimization

Designing compelling and visually appealing ads is crucial for capturing users' attention and driving engagement. To optimize your ad creative and maximize its impact, consider the following best practices:

Keep it Simple and Clear: Aim for simplicity in your ad design. Communicate your message clearly and concisely to ensure that users understand your offering at a glance. Avoid cluttered visuals or excessive text that may overwhelm viewers.

Use High-Quality Visuals: Choose high-resolution images or videos that are relevant to your brand and campaign. High-quality visuals not only enhance the overall aesthetic of your ad but also reflect the professionalism and credibility of your brand.

Incorporate Branding Elements: Consistently include your brand's logo, colors, and fonts in your ad creative. This reinforces brand recognition and helps users associate the ad with your brand. Maintain a cohesive visual identity across your ads to establish brand consistency.

Create a Strong Call-to-Action (CTA): Include a clear and compelling CTA that prompts users to take the desired action. Use action-oriented language such as "Shop Now," "Learn More," or "Sign Up." Place the CTA prominently and make it visually distinct from the rest of the ad.

Optimize for Mobile: Given the increasing mobile usage, ensure your ad creative is mobile-friendly. Use vertical or square formats for images and videos to maximize visibility on mobile screens. Test your ads across different devices and screen sizes to ensure a seamless user experience.

Test Multiple Variations: Experiment with different versions of your ad creative to identify the most effective elements. Test variations in headlines, visuals, CTAs, or ad formats to understand which combinations resonate best with your audience.

A/B testing can provide valuable insights for optimizing your ads.

Consider Emotional Appeal: Emotions can play a powerful role in ad effectiveness. Craft your ad creative to evoke emotions such as joy, excitement, or empathy. Emotional connections can make your ads more memorable and increase the likelihood of user engagement.

Maintain Relevance: Align your ad creative with the target audience and the platform you're using. Consider the interests, preferences, and behaviors of your audience to create relevant and personalized ads. Tailor your messaging and visuals to resonate with your specific target audience.

Follow Platform Guidelines: Adhere to the ad specifications and guidelines provided by the social media platform. Each platform has specific requirements for image dimensions, video lengths, text limits, and other elements. By following these guidelines, you can ensure your ads are displayed correctly and reach their intended audience.

Monitor Performance and Iterate: Regularly monitor the performance of your ads and gather insights from analytics data. Identify what works and what doesn't, and use these insights to refine and optimize your ad creative. Continuously iterate and experiment to improve the effectiveness of your campaigns.

By implementing these best practices, you can create visually appealing, engaging, and optimized ad creative that effectively communicates your message and drives desired actions from your target audience. Remember to stay up to date with design trends and evolving consumer preferences to ensure your ads remain fresh and impactful.

Implementing Tracking Pixels and Conversion Tracking

Tracking pixels and conversion tracking are essential tools in social media advertising that allow you to measure and analyze the effectiveness of your campaigns. By implementing tracking pixels and setting up conversion tracking, you can gain valuable insights into user behavior, optimize your ad performance, and track the success of your advertising efforts. Here's an overview of how to implement tracking pixels and utilize conversion tracking:

Tracking Pixels:
A tracking pixel is a small piece of code provided by social media platforms that you place on your website. It allows you to track user interactions and conversions that result from your ads.

To implement a tracking pixel, you typically need to place the pixel code on specific pages of your website, such as the purchase confirmation page or a lead generation form submission page.
Once the tracking pixel is in place, it will track actions taken by users who click on your ads and visit your website. This data helps you measure the effectiveness of your campaigns, such as the number of website visits, conversions, or specific actions taken by users.

Conversion Tracking:
Conversion tracking goes hand in hand with tracking pixels and allows you to measure and attribute specific actions or conversions to your ads.
Determine the actions or events you want to track as conversions, such as purchases, form submissions, app downloads, or newsletter sign-ups.
Set up conversion tracking within the social media advertising platform by

specifying the conversion event and providing relevant details, such as the conversion value, currency, or specific parameters.

Once conversion tracking is implemented, you can track the number of conversions, their value, and other related metrics. This information helps you evaluate the success of your campaigns and optimize your advertising strategy.

Analyzing and Optimizing:
Regularly analyze the data from tracking pixels and conversion tracking to gain insights into the performance of your ads and campaigns.

Monitor key metrics such as click-through rates (CTR), conversion rates, cost per conversion, and return on ad spend (ROAS).

Identify high-performing campaigns, ad sets, or ad variations, and allocate more budget towards them to maximize results.

Use the data to refine your targeting, ad creative, and messaging to improve overall campaign performance.

Consider using A/B testing to compare different ad variations and identify the most effective elements for driving conversions.

Continuously optimize your campaigns based on the insights gained from tracking pixels and conversion tracking to achieve better results and improve your return on investment (ROI).

Implementing tracking pixels and conversion tracking is a crucial step in understanding the impact of your social media advertising efforts. By accurately tracking user behavior and attributing conversions to specific ads, you can make data-driven decisions, optimize your campaigns, and achieve your advertising goals effectively.

Monitoring Key Performance Metrics (KPIs) and Campaign Success

Monitoring key performance metrics (KPIs) is vital for assessing the success of your social media advertising campaigns. By regularly tracking and analyzing relevant metrics, you can gain insights into the effectiveness of your campaigns, make data-driven decisions, and optimize your advertising strategy. Here are some key steps to monitor KPIs and evaluate campaign success:

Define Your KPIs:
Start by identifying the key metrics that align with your advertising goals and objectives. These KPIs should reflect the desired outcomes you want to achieve with your campaigns.
Common social media advertising KPIs include click-through rate (CTR), conversion rate, cost per click (CPC), cost per acquisition (CPA),

return on ad spend (ROAS), engagement rate, reach, and impressions.

Choose KPIs that are relevant to your specific campaign goals, whether it's driving website traffic, increasing conversions, or boosting brand awareness.

Set Benchmarks and Goals:
Establish benchmarks or baseline metrics based on past campaign performance or industry standards. These benchmarks provide a reference point for evaluating your current campaigns.

Set specific goals for each KPI that align with your overall advertising objectives. Ensure your goals are realistic, measurable, and time-bound to track progress effectively.

Track and Analyze Metrics:
Utilize the analytics tools provided by the social media platforms to track and measure your selected KPIs. These tools

offer insights into ad performance, audience engagement, and other relevant metrics.

Regularly monitor the performance of your campaigns and track the metrics over time. Look for patterns, trends, or significant changes that can inform your optimization strategies.

Analyze the data to identify areas of improvement and opportunities for optimization. For example, if you notice a low conversion rate, you might consider adjusting your targeting, ad creative, or landing page to enhance performance.

Compare and Iterate:
Compare the performance of different campaigns, ad sets, or ad variations to identify the most effective strategies. Determine which elements contribute to better results and use that knowledge to refine your future campaigns.

Conduct A/B testing by running multiple variations of your ads and comparing their performance. This helps you identify the winning elements and optimize your creative and messaging. Continuously iterate and refine your campaigns based on the insights gained from monitoring KPIs. Make data-driven decisions and adjust your targeting, ad creative, or budget allocation to improve campaign success.

Reporting and Communication: Generate regular reports summarizing the performance of your campaigns. Include key metrics, trends, and insights that provide a clear picture of the campaign's effectiveness. Communicate the results with stakeholders, such as your team members, clients, or management. Highlight the achievements, areas for improvement, and recommendations for future campaigns.

By monitoring key performance metrics and evaluating campaign success, you can optimize your social media advertising efforts, make informed decisions, and achieve better results. Regularly tracking and analyzing KPIs provide valuable insights that help you refine your strategies, increase ROI, and drive meaningful business outcomes.

Using Analytics Tools to Gain Insights and Make Data-Driven Decisions

Analytics tools play a crucial role in social media advertising, enabling you to gather valuable data and gain insights into the performance of your campaigns. By leveraging these tools, you can make informed, data-driven decisions that optimize your advertising strategy and drive better results. Here's how you can effectively use analytics tools to gain insights and make data-driven decisions:

Choose the Right Analytics Tools: Select analytics tools that are compatible with the social media platforms you are using for advertising. Most platforms provide built-in analytics dashboards, such as Facebook Insights, Twitter Analytics, or LinkedIn Analytics. Additionally, consider using third-party analytics tools that offer advanced features and cross-platform insights, such as Google Analytics or social media management platforms like Hootsuite or Sprout Social.

Set Up Conversion and Event Tracking:
Implement tracking pixels and conversion tracking codes on your website to track user actions and conversions driven by your social media ads.
Define conversion events, such as purchases, form submissions, or app downloads, and configure the tracking tools to measure and attribute those conversions to your ads.

Track Key Metrics:
Identify the key performance metrics (KPIs) that align with your advertising goals. These may include click-through rate (CTR), conversion rate, engagement rate, reach, impressions, or return on ad spend (ROAS).

Regularly monitor and track these metrics using your analytics tools to measure the performance and effectiveness of your campaigns.

Analyze Data and Identify Insights: Dive into the data provided by the analytics tools to gain insights into user behavior, audience demographics, engagement patterns, and campaign performance.
Analyze trends, patterns, and correlations within the data to identify what is working and what needs improvement. Look for opportunities to optimize your targeting, messaging, ad creative, or budget allocation.

Segment and Compare Data: Utilize the segmentation capabilities of your analytics tools to dissect the data by different dimensions, such as audience demographics, geographic location, or device types.

Compare the performance of different ad sets, campaigns, or variations to understand which strategies are generating the best results. Identify the high-performing segments and replicate their success in future campaigns.

Make Data-Driven Decisions:
Base your decisions on the insights derived from the analytics data rather than relying solely on assumptions or guesswork.
Use the data to refine your targeting, optimize your ad creative, allocate budget strategically, or adjust your campaign strategy to align with the audience's preferences and behaviors.

Test and Iterate:
Implement A/B testing to experiment with different ad variations, targeting options, or messaging strategies. Use the analytics data to evaluate the performance of these variations and iterate accordingly.

Continuously test, learn, and refine your campaigns based on the insights gained from analytics tools. This iterative approach allows you to continually improve your advertising efforts.

Generate Reports and Communicate Findings:

Create regular reports summarizing the key findings, trends, and performance metrics. These reports help you communicate the results to stakeholders, such as team members, clients, or management.

Present the insights in a clear and actionable manner, highlighting the successes, areas for improvement, and recommendations for future campaigns. By leveraging analytics tools effectively, you can gain valuable insights into your social media advertising campaigns. The data and insights obtained through these tools empower you to make informed decisions, optimize your strategies, and drive better results in your advertising efforts.

Importance of A/B Testing in Social Media Advertising

A/B testing is a crucial technique in social media advertising that allows advertisers to compare and optimize different variations of their ads, targeting, and strategies. It involves testing two or more variations of an element to determine which performs better in terms of achieving the desired goals. A/B testing holds significant importance in social media advertising for the following reasons:

Data-Driven Decision Making:

A/B testing enables advertisers to make data-driven decisions rather than relying on assumptions or guesswork. By testing different variations, advertisers can gather empirical evidence about what works and what doesn't, helping them make informed choices based on actual performance data.

Performance Optimization:
A/B testing helps optimize the performance of social media advertising campaigns. It allows advertisers to identify the most effective ad elements, such as headlines, images, ad copy, or calls-to-action (CTAs), by comparing their impact on key metrics like click-through rate (CTR), conversion rate, engagement rate, or return on ad spend (ROAS). Optimizing these elements can lead to improved campaign results and higher ROI.

Audience Insights:
Through A/B testing, advertisers gain valuable insights into their target audience's preferences and behaviors. By testing different targeting options, advertisers can understand which audience segments respond better to their ads, allowing them to refine their

targeting strategies and tailor their messaging to specific customer segments.

Continuous Improvement:
A/B testing promotes a culture of continuous improvement in social media advertising. It encourages advertisers to experiment with new ideas, creative concepts, and strategies while collecting data on their performance. By continually testing and iterating, advertisers can refine their campaigns, discover new opportunities, and stay ahead of the competition.

Cost Efficiency:
A/B testing helps advertisers allocate their resources more efficiently. By identifying the highest-performing variations, advertisers can allocate more budget to those elements, ensuring that their ad spend is focused on strategies that deliver the best results.

This optimization helps minimize wasted ad spend on ineffective approaches and maximizes the efficiency of advertising budgets.

Adapting to Audience Preferences:
A/B testing allows advertisers to adapt their messaging and creative elements to align with the preferences and tastes of their target audience. By testing different variations, advertisers can determine which elements resonate better with their audience, enabling them to create more relevant and engaging ad experiences.

Staying Competitive:
In the dynamic landscape of social media advertising, staying competitive is essential. A/B testing allows advertisers to stay on top of industry trends and evolving audience preferences.

By regularly testing and iterating their campaigns, advertisers can ensure their strategies remain effective and adjust their approaches to match changing market dynamics.

Testing Different Ad Variations and Targeting Options

Testing different ad variations and targeting options is a fundamental aspect of social media advertising. By experimenting with various ad elements and targeting strategies, advertisers can uncover insights and optimize their campaigns to maximize performance and achieve their advertising goals. In this section, we will explore the importance of testing ad variations and targeting options and provide guidelines for effective testing.

Ad Variations Testing:
Test different ad variations to identify the elements that resonate best with your audience.
Experiment with variations in ad copy, headlines, calls-to-action (CTAs), visuals, and ad formats.
Test different messaging approaches, such as highlighting product features, emphasizing benefits, or using social proof.
Measure the performance of each variation based on key metrics like click-through rate (CTR), conversion rate, or engagement rate.

Targeting Options Testing:
Test different targeting options to find the most effective audience segments for your ads.

Experiment with variations in demographics, interests, behaviors, or location targeting.
Create separate ad sets or campaigns targeting different audience segments and compare their performance.
Analyze the metrics to identify the segments that deliver the highest engagement and conversions.

A/B Testing Methodology:
Define a clear hypothesis for each test. What specific outcome or improvement do you expect from the test?
Determine the variables you want to test, whether it's ad variations, targeting options, or a combination of both.
Set up control groups and test groups to ensure an accurate comparison between variations.
Allocate a sufficient budget and run the test for an appropriate duration to gather statistically significant data.
Monitor and measure the performance of each variation using relevant metrics.

Analyze the results and draw insights to inform your optimization strategy.

Analyzing Test Results:
Compare the performance of different ad variations and targeting options based on the defined metrics.
Look for statistically significant differences in performance to identify winning variations.
Consider both short-term and long-term performance to assess the impact on overall campaign success.
Use data analysis tools and platforms provided by social media advertising platforms to gain insights and visualize the results.

Iterative Optimization:
Implement the insights gained from the testing phase to optimize your campaigns.
Apply the winning variations to your ongoing or future campaigns to improve their performance.

Continuously test new variations and refine your strategies to adapt to changing audience preferences and market dynamics.

Iterate and repeat the testing process regularly to maintain a data-driven approach and optimize results over time. Testing different ad variations and targeting options empowers advertisers to refine their campaigns, improve audience targeting, and optimize their messaging for better performance. By leveraging the insights gained from testing, advertisers can create more engaging ads, enhance their ad relevance, and achieve their desired outcomes in social media advertising.

Iterative Optimization Based on Data Analysis and Audience Response

Iterative optimization is a continuous improvement process in social media advertising that involves analyzing data and audience response to refine and enhance advertising campaigns over time. By leveraging data analysis and monitoring audience engagement, advertisers can make data-driven decisions, uncover valuable insights, and optimize their strategies for better results. In this section, we will explore the importance of iterative optimization and provide guidelines for implementing it effectively.

Data Analysis:
Regularly analyze the performance metrics of your social media advertising campaigns.
Use analytics tools provided by the social media platforms or third-party software to gather relevant data.

Identify key performance indicators (KPIs) such as click-through rate (CTR), conversion rate, engagement rate, or return on ad spend (ROAS).
Analyze the data to understand how different elements of your campaigns contribute to these metrics.

Audience Response Monitoring:
Monitor audience engagement and response to your ads.
Track user interactions, comments, shares, and feedback on social media platforms.
Pay attention to qualitative feedback and sentiment expressed by the audience.
Listen to your audience's preferences, needs, and pain points to inform your optimization strategy.

Identifying Patterns and Trends:
Look for patterns and trends in the data to identify areas of improvement.
Determine which ad variations, targeting options, or messaging approaches are

performing well and which are underperforming.

Identify common characteristics of the audience segments that engage most effectively with your ads.

Explore trends over time and compare results across different campaigns or time periods.

Hypothesis and Experimentation:
Develop hypotheses based on the insights gained from data analysis and audience response.

Formulate ideas and strategies to address the areas of improvement identified in the data.

Experiment with new ad variations, targeting options, or creative approaches to validate your hypotheses.

Implement A/B testing or multivariate testing to compare the performance of different variations and gather empirical evidence.

Measurement and Evaluation:
Measure the performance of your experiments and compare the results with the baseline metrics.
Assess the impact of the changes on the identified KPIs and evaluate the success of your optimization efforts.
Consider both short-term and long-term effects to determine the overall effectiveness of the optimizations.

Implementation and Scaling:
Implement the successful optimizations across your campaigns and scale them to reach a larger audience.
Continuously monitor and analyze the performance of the optimized campaigns to ensure they maintain their effectiveness.
Regularly review and iterate your optimization strategy based on the changing needs and preferences of your audience.

Iterative optimization based on data analysis and audience response is an ongoing process that allows advertisers to refine their social media advertising campaigns and maximize their impact. By continuously monitoring and analyzing data, experimenting with new strategies, and implementing successful optimizations, advertisers can adapt to their audience's needs, stay ahead of the competition, and achieve better results in their social media advertising endeavors.

Strategies for Scaling Successful Campaigns

Scaling successful campaigns in social media advertising is crucial for reaching a larger audience, increasing brand exposure, and driving better results. When a campaign proves to be effective, it's important to capitalize on its success and expand its reach. In this section, we will explore strategies for scaling successful campaigns effectively.

Increase Budget Allocation:

Allocate a larger budget to your successful campaigns to increase their reach and frequency.

Consider reallocating funds from underperforming campaigns or experimenting with a higher budget to maximize the impact of your successful campaigns.

Monitor the performance closely to ensure the increased budget is generating the desired results.

Expand Targeting Options:
Identify additional audience segments or demographics that align with the success of your campaign.
Extend your targeting options to include new demographics, interests, or behaviors that are likely to respond positively to your campaign.
Leverage audience insights and data analysis to refine your targeting strategies and expand your reach.

Explore New Platforms:
Identify other social media platforms that are popular among your target audience.
Expand your campaign to reach audiences on different platforms, leveraging the unique features and user behaviors of each platform.

Adapt your creative and messaging to suit the specific platform while maintaining consistency with your overall brand identity.

Utilize Advanced Targeting Options: Take advantage of advanced targeting options provided by social media advertising platforms.
Explore options such as lookalike audiences, custom audiences, or retargeting to reach users who are similar to your existing audience or have shown interest in your brand.
Refine your targeting by combining multiple options to create highly specific audience segments.

Experiment with New Ad Formats: Test new ad formats and placements to diversify your campaign's reach and impact.
Consider using video ads, carousel ads, or interactive ads to capture users' attention and increase engagement.

Monitor the performance of the new ad formats and optimize accordingly to ensure they align with your campaign goals.

Collaborate with Influencers or Partners:
Partner with influencers or complementary brands to extend the reach of your successful campaigns. Collaborate with influencers who have a significant following in your target market to amplify your brand message. Leverage the credibility and reach of influencers or partners to expand your campaign's visibility and connect with new audiences.

Optimize Landing Pages and Conversion Funnel:
Ensure that your landing pages and conversion funnel are optimized to handle increased traffic and conversions.

Conduct A/B testing on landing pages, CTAs, and user experience to improve conversion rates.
Implement remarketing strategies to re-engage users who have shown interest but haven't converted yet.

Continuously Monitor and Optimize: Maintain a close eye on the performance of your scaled campaigns.
Regularly analyze data, monitor metrics, and identify areas for further optimization.
Make data-driven decisions and iterate your strategies based on the insights gained.
Scaling successful campaigns requires a strategic and data-driven approach. By increasing budgets, expanding targeting options, exploring new platforms and ad formats, collaborating with influencers, optimizing the conversion funnel, and monitoring performance closely, advertisers can effectively extend the reach and impact of their successful

campaigns. It's essential to continuously test, refine, and optimize your strategies to ensure sustained growth and maximize the return on investment.

Exploring Advanced Targeting Options and Features

In social media advertising, advanced targeting options and features offer advertisers the opportunity to refine their audience targeting strategies and optimize campaign performance. By leveraging these advanced capabilities, advertisers can reach the most relevant and receptive audience segments, leading to higher engagement and conversions.

In this section, we will explore various advanced targeting options and features that can enhance your social media advertising efforts.

Lookalike Audiences:
Lookalike audiences allow you to reach new users who share similarities with your existing customers or audience. Social media platforms analyze the characteristics, interests, and behaviors of your current audience and identify users who closely resemble them.
By targeting lookalike audiences, you can expand your reach to users who are likely to be interested in your products or services.

Custom Audiences:
Custom audiences enable you to target specific groups of users based on your own customer data.
Upload your customer email lists, phone numbers, or user IDs to the social media

platform, which matches them to user accounts.

This targeting option allows you to re-engage existing customers, target high-value prospects, or create personalized messaging for specific segments.

Retargeting:
Retargeting allows you to re-engage users who have previously interacted with your brand or visited your website. Implement tracking pixels or cookies to track user behavior and show tailored ads to users who have shown interest in your brand.

This targeting option helps to remind users of your brand, encourage them to complete conversions, or drive repeat purchases.

Behavioral Targeting:
Behavioral targeting focuses on reaching users based on their online behaviors and interests.

Social media platforms analyze user behavior, such as pages liked, content engaged with, or apps used, to identify relevant audience segments.
By targeting users with specific behaviors, you can align your ads with their interests and increase the likelihood of engagement.

Interest-Based Targeting:
Interest-based targeting enables you to target users based on their expressed interests and preferences.
Social media platforms collect data on users' likes, shares, and interactions to understand their interests.
This targeting option allows you to deliver ads to users who have indicated an interest in topics related to your products or services.

Geo-Targeting:
Geo-targeting allows you to target users based on their geographical location.

Define specific regions, cities, or even zip codes to ensure your ads are shown to users in the desired location.
This targeting option is particularly useful for businesses with a local or regional focus.

Demographic Targeting:
Demographic targeting allows you to reach users based on their demographic characteristics, such as age, gender, education, or income level.
Tailor your ad content and messaging to resonate with specific demographic groups.
This targeting option helps you focus your budget on reaching the audience most likely to be interested in your offerings.

Contextual Targeting:
Contextual targeting involves displaying ads on social media platforms in relation to specific content or keywords.

Align your ads with relevant topics, discussions, or trending keywords to increase their relevance and visibility. This targeting option ensures that your ads are displayed to users who are actively engaged in content related to your offerings.

When exploring advanced targeting options and features, it's essential to align them with your campaign goals and target audience. Experiment with different combinations of targeting options, analyze the results, and optimize your strategy based on data-driven insights. By leveraging advanced targeting capabilities, you can refine your audience targeting, improve relevance, and enhance the effectiveness of your social media advertising campaigns.

Expanding Your Reach Across Multiple Social Media Platforms

Expanding your reach across multiple social media platforms is a strategic approach to broaden your audience, increase brand visibility, and maximize the impact of your advertising efforts. Each social media platform has its own unique user base, features, and engagement patterns. By diversifying your presence across multiple platforms, you can tap into different demographics, interests, and behaviors, reaching a wider range of potential customers. Here are some key considerations and benefits of expanding your reach across multiple social media platforms:

Reach a Diverse Audience:
Different social media platforms attract diverse user demographics and interests. By expanding your presence, you can connect with users who may not be

active on other platforms, ensuring your message reaches a broader audience. This allows you to engage with a more diverse range of potential customers and expand your brand's reach.

Amplify Brand Awareness:
Being present on multiple platforms increases your brand's visibility and exposure.
It creates more touchpoints with your target audience, increasing the likelihood of them encountering your brand and messaging.
The repetition and consistency of your brand across multiple platforms help reinforce brand recall and recognition.

Leverage Platform-Specific Features:
Each social media platform offers unique features and tools that can enhance your advertising efforts.
By expanding to multiple platforms, you can leverage specific features such as Instagram Stories, Twitter hashtags,

LinkedIn professional networking, or YouTube video ads.
Utilizing platform-specific features enables you to tailor your content and creative to the platform's strengths, maximizing engagement and effectiveness.

Adapt to User Behavior:
Users have different behaviors and preferences across social media platforms.
Expanding your reach allows you to align with the preferred communication style and content consumption habits of users on each platform.
For example, Instagram users may prefer visual content, while Twitter users may appreciate concise and timely messages.
Adapting your content and approach to each platform helps you connect more effectively with users and generate better engagement.

Improve Cross-Platform Consistency:
Expanding across multiple platforms
enables you to maintain a consistent
brand presence and messaging across
different channels.
Consistency builds trust, reinforces
brand identity, and enhances the overall
user experience.
Ensure your branding elements, tone of
voice, and messaging align across all
platforms to create a cohesive and
recognizable brand image.

Test and Optimize Performance:
Having a presence on multiple platforms
allows you to compare performance and
identify the most effective platforms for
your specific goals.
You can conduct A/B testing and
experiment with different ad formats,
messaging, and targeting options on
each platform.

Analyze the performance metrics and insights to refine your strategy, optimize campaigns, and allocate resources to the platforms that generate the best results.

Stay Ahead of the Competition:
Expanding across multiple platforms helps you stay competitive in the ever-evolving digital landscape.
It allows you to reach users who may be exclusive to certain platforms or who prefer different platforms than your competitors.
By diversifying your presence, you can gain a competitive advantage, attract new customers, and establish a strong brand presence across various channels.
When expanding your reach across multiple social media platforms, it's important to consider your target audience, goals, and available resources.

Prioritize platforms that align with your audience demographics and behavior, and ensure you have the capacity to maintain an active and engaging presence on each platform. By effectively managing your presence across multiple platforms, you can amplify your brand's reach, engage with a diverse audience, and drive better results from your social media advertising efforts.

Conclusion

Social media advertising offers immense opportunities for businesses to reach and engage their target audience effectively. In this guide, we have explored various aspects of social media advertising, starting from understanding its power to setting goals, identifying target audiences, crafting compelling ad content, selecting the right platforms, managing budgets and bidding strategies, creating and launching ads, tracking and analyzing performance, conducting A/B testing, scaling campaigns, and exploring advanced targeting options.

By harnessing the power of social media advertising, businesses can benefit from its wide reach, precise targeting capabilities, and interactive nature.

The ability to connect with users on platforms they actively use and engage with presents a unique opportunity to build brand awareness, drive website traffic, generate leads, and boost conversions.

It is crucial to align your advertising goals and objectives with the capabilities of social media platforms. Setting SMART goals ensures that your campaigns are focused, measurable, achievable, relevant, and time-bound. Defining your target audience demographics and conducting market research provides valuable insights for effective audience segmentation and personalized messaging.

Crafting engaging ad content, including compelling copy and captivating visuals, is vital to capture users' attention and evoke a desired response.

Choosing the right social media platforms that align with your target audience's demographics and user behavior is essential for maximizing your reach and impact.

Managing budgets, understanding bidding strategies, and optimizing campaigns based on data analysis are crucial for maximizing return on investment (ROI) and minimizing costs. Tracking key performance metrics, implementing tracking pixels, and using analytics tools enable you to monitor campaign performance, gain insights, and make data-driven decisions for continuous improvement.

A/B testing and iterative optimization play a pivotal role in refining your advertising strategies. Testing different ad variations, targeting options, and creative elements helps you identify the most effective approaches and optimize your campaigns for better results.

Scaling successful campaigns and exploring advanced targeting options allow you to expand your reach and connect with a broader audience. By leveraging platform-specific features, adapting to user behavior, and maintaining consistency across multiple social media platforms, you can enhance your brand's visibility, engagement, and competitiveness.

In conclusion, social media advertising has become an integral part of the marketing landscape. Understanding its power, setting clear goals, identifying your target audience, creating compelling content, selecting the right platforms, tracking performance, conducting tests, and optimizing campaigns are key to achieving success in social media advertising.

By continually refining your strategies and staying up to date with the latest trends and features, you can harness the full potential of social media advertising and drive meaningful results for your business.